UNIT 17

5   6   7   8   9   RRD   14   13   12   11   10

Read Well is a registered trademark of Sopris West Educational Services.

ISBN 978-1-60218-556-2
ISBN 1-60218-556-5

Printed in the United States of America
Published and Distributed by

Cambium
LEARNING®
Sopris West®

4093 Specialty Place • Longmont, CO 80504 • (303) 651-2829
www.sopriswest.com

167302/1-10

SCIENCE & LITERATURE

FOR KIDS

Volume 1 | Number 1

The *Read Well Science Digest* is a new feature of the *Read Well* reading program, published by Sopris West, a division of Cambium Learning.

Note: See the Unit 17 Teacher's Guide for Lesson Planning.

4

Letter From the Editor

Dear Readers:

All living things need energy to survive. That energy comes from food. For people, food can be many different things—roast beef, salads, a taco, rice, watermelon, or oatmeal. Humans get very fancy with their meals and cook all kinds of scrumptious things.

For most living things, food is much simpler. Most animals just eat other living things. These animals and the plants they eat are connected in what is called a food chain.

This issue of *Read Well Science Digest* is all about food chains.

Enjoy!
Guest Editor
Professor Worm

VOCABULARY POWER! 1

★ **en·er·gy**

Energy is the power to do things.

Eating the right kinds of foods gives us *energy*. We need energy to think. What else do we need energy to do?

★ **con·nect**

Connect means to join two or more things.

She *connected* the hose to the faucet. How do you connect the hose to the faucet?

★ **link**

A **link** is something that connects two things.

The rings in a chain are *links*. How many links are in the chain?

★ = New

her·bi·vore

An **herbivore** is an animal that eats only plants.

A rabbit is an herbivore. What does a rabbit eat?

car·ni·vore

A **carnivore** is an animal that eats mostly meat.

A wolf is a carnivore. What does a wolf eat?

Links in the Chain

by L.J. Sellers

Food chains are everywhere.

Grass grows in a meadow.
A deer grazes on the grass.
Then a cougar kills and eats the deer.

The grass, deer, and cougar are connected in a food chain. Grass gets energy from the sun. The deer gets energy from the grass. The cougar gets energy from the deer.

Sun

Grass

Deer

Cougar

Look at the picture. Explain how the grass, deer, and cougar are connected in a food chain.

What do you think would happen if the deer had no grass to eat? What would happen to the cougar if there were no deer to eat?

Why are living things important to one another?

9

Green Plants

Green plants are the first link in the food chain. These plants are special because they make their own food. They use water, sunlight, and air to make the food they need.

Green plants are everywhere. There are millions, billions, and trillions of plants. This is a good thing, because animals eat lots and lots of plants.

Why are green plants important?

Plant Eaters

Plant eaters are the second link in the food chain. They come in all shapes and sizes. Tiny brown rabbits, mid-size brown deer, and enormous gray elephants are all plant eaters. Plant eaters live in forests, grasslands, rain forests, and oceans. Plant eaters are called herbivores.

What is the same about all herbivores?

Meat Eaters

Meat eaters—like eagles, wolves, and sharks—are at the top of the food chain. They eat other animals and are called carnivores. But carnivores have to watch out too. Some carnivores eat other carnivores.

Why do carnivores have to watch out too?

In an ocean food chain, tiny plants are eaten by fish. Then the fish may be eaten by a seal. The seal is a carnivore, but it may be eaten by a killer whale.

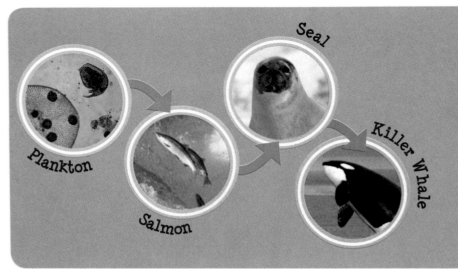

Plankton

Salmon

Seal

Killer Whale

A Food Chain Puzzle

Build a food chain from the following living things:
a cat, a caterpillar, a leaf, a robin.

Caterpillar

Cat

Leaf

Robin

1 Point to the first link in the food chain.

2 Point to the second link.

3 Point to the third link.

4 Point to the fourth link. This animal is at the top of this food chain.

Describe this food chain.

12

What's Not Right?

o Herbivores love me.
o I get energy from the sun.
o I am a treat for carnivores.

o I love to eat meat.
o An owl would like me for lunch.
o I am an herbivore.

o I love to eat plants.
o I get energy from eating small animals.
o I am a carnivore.

From Grass to Meatballs

by Susan Blackaby

As the first link in the food chain, green plants are very important. Without green plants, there would be no meatballs. What? You say no meatballs! How can that be?

Follow the chain:

2 Cattle eat the grass.

1 The grass makes food, using energy from the sun.

Without green plants, what would happen to your meatballs? Without grass, the cattle would starve. Without cattle, there would be no meat to package. Without meat, there would be no meatballs.

So the next time you see green grass in a field, think meatballs and say "Thank you."

3 The butcher packages and sells the meat.

4 You and your family make meatballs from a package of that meat.

Why are green plants needed for meatballs?

15

VOCABULARY POWER! 2

★ u·nique

Unique means very special and one of a kind.

Each person has fingerprints that are different. No one has fingerprints that are the same. Fingerprints are . . .

pred·a·tor

A **predator** is an animal that hunts other animals for food.

A spider is a *predator* that kills and eats insects. What makes an animal a predator?

★ no·mad·ic

Nomadic describes people or animals that move around and do not stay in one place for very long.

Some American Indians lived a *nomadic* life because they followed the buffalo. What did they do when they followed the buffalo?

scarce

When something is **scarce**, there is not enough for everyone.

The land was dry. Few plants could grow because water was . . .

★ = New

16

prey

Prey is an animal that is hunted and eaten by another animal.

Rabbits are the *prey* of wolves and other carnivores. What are other kinds of prey?

Now You Try It!

Try defining the next word. Then look up the word in the glossary. Your definition might be better!

★ food chain

Start with "A *food chain* is . . ."
Let's find the word on page 67.

17

WHAT'S BLACK

What's black and white and smiles?

AND WHITE

What's black and white and makes whuffling sounds?

AND LOVED BY ALL?

by Marilyn Sprick

19

It's a Zebra!

A zebra is in the horse family. Like a horse, a zebra whinnies, grazes, and runs like the wind. Zebras also bray and make strange snorting, whuffling sounds. Of course, a zebra is black and white and has stripes.

What's With the Stripes?

Every zebra has its own pattern of stripes. Zebras use these unique patterns to recognize one another. Look carefully. Can you tell the difference between the two zebras? What is unique about each zebra's stripes?

Name three facts about a zebra.

21

Quiz

If you shaved a zebra, what do you think you would find?

a) white skin
b) black skin
c) striped skin
d) pink skin

What's your best guess? The answer is on page 25.

Zebras in the Food Chain

Grass is the first link in the zebra's food chain. Zebras are the second link. They are nomadic herbivores. They travel around in search of fresh grass and water.

Lions are the next link in the food chain. These carnivores wait at the water holes for the zebras. Zebras know when lions are nearby, but water is often scarce and the zebras must drink.

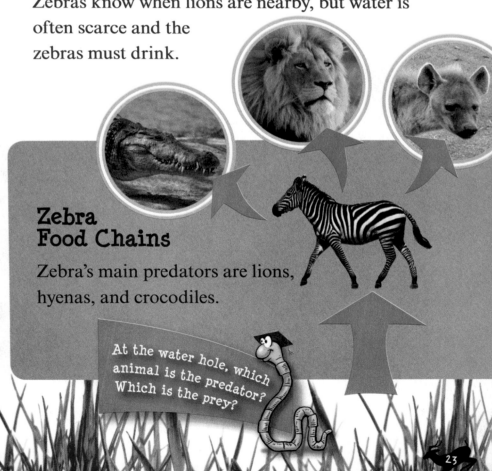

Zebra Food Chains

Zebra's main predators are lions, hyenas, and crocodiles.

At the water hole, which animal is the predator? Which is the prey?

Protection

At the water hole, zebras must watch for predators, and they do. They must listen, and they do. When a lion is near, all the animals at the water hole must be on the lookout.

If zebras spot a lion, what should they do?

Zebras defend themselves by kicking and biting, but their best protection is to run. When a lion is spotted, the zebras bark a warning and then race away.

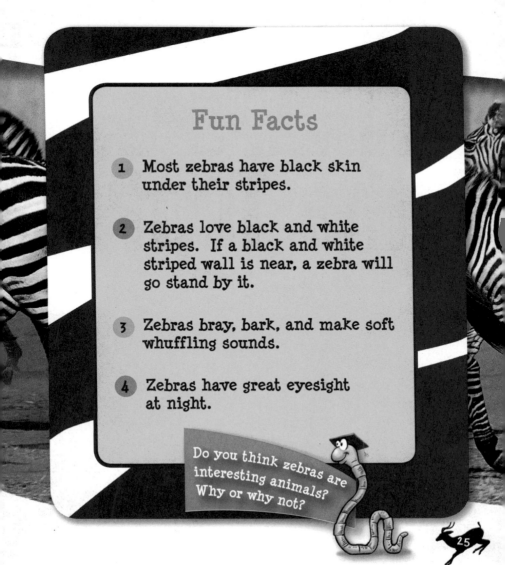

Fun Facts

1. Most zebras have black skin under their stripes.

2. Zebras love black and white stripes. If a black and white striped wall is near, a zebra will go stand by it.

3. Zebras bray, bark, and make soft whuffling sounds.

4. Zebras have great eyesight at night.

Do you think zebras are interesting animals? Why or why not?

What's at the Top?

by Marilyn Sprick

Who

am

I?

27

A Lion!

A lion is in the cat family. It meows. It hisses. It snarls and roars. When a lion roars, it can be heard from five miles away. A lion is at the top of the food chain. He is often called the king of beasts.

Why is a lion called the king of beasts?

Lions in the Food Chain

On the African grasslands, lions are at the top of the food chain. The grazers—zebras, impalas, buffalo, and giraffes—eat plants. Then these herbivores are food for the lions.

Quiz

If you were a lion, would you:

a) hunt all day?
b) take short naps?
c) sleep 21 hours a day?
d) go to the movies?

The answer is on page 34.

29

Teamwork

Lions live in families called prides. When the pride is hungry, the female cats hunt. At night or in the early morning, the big cats go in search of large mammals—buffalo, zebras, or antelopes.

When a lioness spots a herd of animals, for example, she huffs to let the others know. The other lionesses quickly crouch down. They move through the dry grass, closer and closer to their prey.

What is a lion family called? How does a lioness communicate with other lionesses during a hunt?

When they get close to the herd, some of the lionesses move into the open. Members of the herd see the big cats and warn the others.

In the meantime, other lionesses move behind the herd. From behind, these cats pounce.

While the other animals in the herd run for their lives, the lionesses work together to bring down a single animal. Within minutes, the lions have a meal.

Explain how the lionesses use teamwork to bring down their prey.

Learning to Hunt

When lion cubs are young, they play. They explore. They crouch. They pounce. They wrestle. In this way, the young lions learn the skills they need for hunting.

Once the lions are more than a year old, they go on hunts with their mothers. By age two, the lions are hunting small animals. At first, they make many mistakes. It is hard for the young lions to wait. The young lions often strike too soon, and their meals run away!

But lions are intelligent. They learn from their mistakes, and they watch their mothers. Before long, the young lions are helping feed their pride.

Name three ways a lion cub learns to hunt.

What makes lions intelligent animals?

A Cub's
First Growl

Cubs
Wrestling

A Cub
Crouching

What Do Lions Do Best of All?

Lions are great sleepers. Lions sleep most of the day and night. In fact, lions may sleep as many as 21 hours in one day. That means these lazy cats may be awake for only three hours. A good snooze is what they do the best!

Name five interesting facts you learned about lions. What fact was the most interesting of all? This article says that lions are intelligent. Do you agree or disagree? Why?

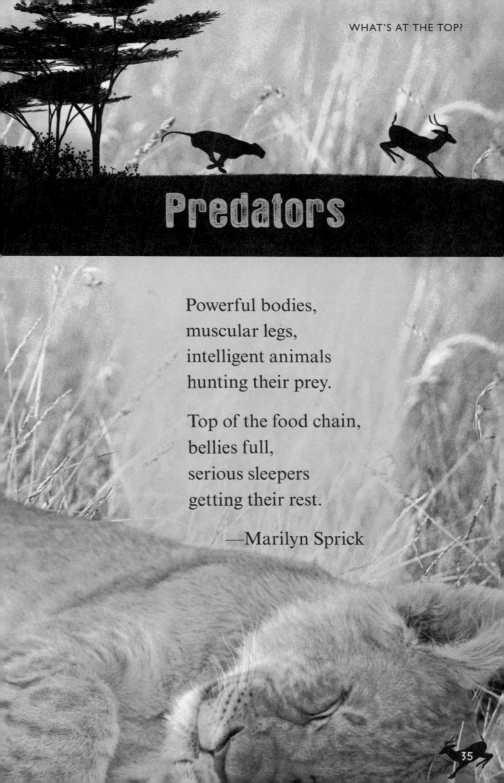

Predators

Powerful bodies,
muscular legs,
intelligent animals
hunting their prey.

Top of the food chain,
bellies full,
serious sleepers
getting their rest.

—Marilyn Sprick

VOCABULARY POWER! 3

★ floss

Floss means to clean between your teeth with a special thread.

The dentist always reminds us to *floss* our teeth. What should we do to keep our teeth and gums healthy?

★ de·cay

Decay means to rot.

When you see black, wet, rotten leaves on the forest floor, what is happening to the leaves? Use your new vocabulary word *decay*.

★ de·com·pos·er

A plant or animal that helps dead matter rot, or decay, is called a **decomposer**.

A mushroom is a *decomposer*. What does it do?

★ di·gest

When your body **digests** food, it breaks it down into energy that you can use.

Your stomach helps you *digest* food. After you eat an apple, what happens to it next?

★ = New

★ re·cy·cle

When you **recycle** something, it can be used again.

We *recycle* paper so it can be used again. What else can you recycle?

Idioms and Expressions

★ ed·u·cat·ed guess

An **educated guess** is not a wild guess. An educated guess is based on facts.

You know that carnivores hunt for their food and eat meat. Make an *educated guess*. Is a cat a carnivore? What facts do you know that helped you make an educated guess?

10 GREAT REASONS TO BE AN EARTHWORM

by Ann Watanabe

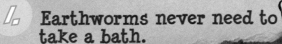

1. Earthworms never need to take a bath.

2. Earthworms never need glasses.

3. Earthworms never get stuffy noses.

4. Earthworms have a lot of heart.

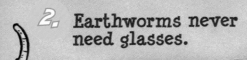

5. Earthworms can grow new tails when their tails get cut off.

6. Earthworms have enormous mouths.

7. Earthworms never have to floss their teeth.

8. Earthworm children get to stay up all night and play in the mud.

9. Earthworms can fool people because their heads and tails look almost the same.

10. The most important reason to be an earthworm: Earthworms take care of the Earth!

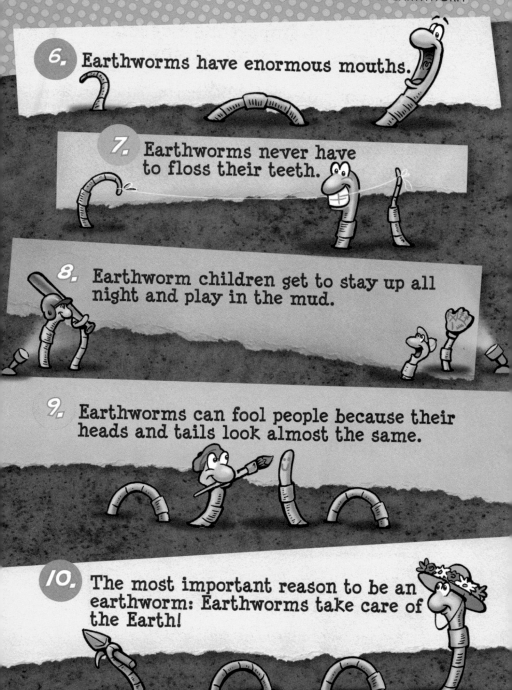

The Most Important Reason It's Great to Be an Earthworm

Earthworms take care of the Earth. They are an important part of the food chain. They eat decaying plants and animals. They are called decomposers. Decomposers change dead stuff into food for plants.

Earthworms use their mouths to pull the dead leaves, grass, seeds, or the remains of dead animals into tunnels in the ground. Earthworms shred the dead matter and then digest it.

Worm Waste

Finally, earthworms leave behind their waste. The waste provides food for plants. It makes the soil rich. Plants grow well in soil that has been tended by earthworms.

Finish these three facts:

Decomposers change dead stuff into . . .

Decomposers make the soil . . .

Decomposers help plants . . .

Make an Educated Guess

What would happen if you planted seeds in two flowerpots, then added worms to the soil in the first pot, but not to the second? If you took care of both pots in the same way, which pot would have bigger, healthier plants?

Wormy but true . . .

Decomposers recycle dead stuff. They turn the dead matter into food for plants.

More About the
10 GREAT REASONS TO BE AN EARTHWORM

by Ann Watanabe

1. Earthworms never need to take a bath.

Earthworm bodies are always wet and slimy. If earthworms dry out, they die. They also die if the ground is too wet. A bath would kill an earthworm. Earthworms work best where the dirt is wet but not too wet.

2. Earthworms never need glasses.

Earthworms don't have eyes! They have cells on their bodies that help them tell the difference between light and dark.

3. Earthworms never get stuffy noses.

Earthworms do not have noses or lungs. They simply breathe through their skin.

4. **Earthworms have a lot of heart.**

Earthworms have ten hearts! The hearts pump blood through the worm's body.

5. **Earthworms can grow new tails.**

Earthworms have a special talent. If you cut off the tail of an earthworm, it can grow a new one.

6. **Earthworms have enormous mouths.**

Earthworms have big mouths—the better to eat and tunnel with, the better to make the soil rich.

7. **Earthworms never have to floss their teeth.**

Earthworms have no teeth! So they don't have to floss or brush.

8. **Earthworm children get to stay up all night and play in the mud.**

The hot sun can dry out a worm, so they don't like the day. At night, worms sometimes come out of their tunnels to find something to eat.

9. **Earthworms can fool people because their heads and tails look almost the same.**

Earthworms have no faces, so it's hard to tell their heads from their tails. Here's the secret. Look for a smooth section. The smooth section is close to the worm's head.

10. **Earthworms take care of the Earth.**

Earthworms are simple creatures, but they have been on Earth for about 300 million years—even before the dinosaurs. Worms keep our plants healthy. They help keep Earth green.

Quiz

True or False

1. Earthworms are great swimmers.

   T F

2. Earthworms have big mouths but no teeth.

   T F

3. Earthworms will ruin your garden!

   T F

4. Earthworms love the hot sun.

   T F

45

VOCABULARY POWER! 4

de·com·pos·er

A plant or animal that helps dead matter rot, or decay, is called a **decomposer**.

An earthworm is a *decomposer*. What does it do?

en·er·gy

Energy is the power to do things.

What gives plants the *energy* to grow?

★ va·cant

Vacant means empty. A building, a room, or even a chair can be vacant.

No one was living in the house. The house was *vacant*. Describe the house in the picture.

★ scur·ry

Scurry means to move quickly with small steps.

The little mouse *scurried* into its hole. Show me how you might scurry across the room.

★ = New

★ thrive

Thrive means to grow and do very well.

If you water a plant and give it sunlight, it will . . .

★ thriv·ing

Something that is **thriving** is growing exceptionally well.

The tomatoes we planted are *thriving* in the sunny garden.

Now You Try It!

Try defining each word. Then look up the word in the glossary. Your definition might be better!

com·mu·ni·ty

Start with "A *community* is . . ."
Let's find the word on page 66.

pred·a·tor

Start with "A *predator* is an animal that . . ."
Let's find the word on page 68.

prey

Start with "*Prey* is an animal that . . ."
Let's find the word on page 68.

Digging Up the Truth

With Professor Worm

Ask Professor Worm your science questions!

Dear Professor Worm,

My brother Dylan and I had a long discussion about you. We have lots of

questions. Are earthworms insects? Can you see in the dark? Can you swim?

PROFESSOR WORM

Ty and Dylan
Hilo, Hawaii

Dear Ty and Dylan,

What excellent questions! Earthworms are not insects! If you want to be scientific, we are annelids. Earthworms cannot see, but we can feel vibrations and sense light. That is how we get around in dark tunnels.

We cannot swim. We would drown if we were even in a puddle. If our tunnels get filled with rainwater, we have to leave.

Sincerely,
Professor Worm

Dear Professor Worm,

What is the difference between a predator and prey? Are you a predator or prey?

Nate J.
Albany, Oregon

Dear Nate,

Such an intelligent question! You must be learning about food chains! An animal that hunts and eats another animal is a predator. Prey is an animal that is eaten.

Earthworms are often eaten by birds. We are prey. Earthworms do not hunt for animals or insects. We are not predators.

Sincerely,
Professor Worm

Dear Professor Worm,

On Saturday, my friend Billy and I went fishing. Billy used earthworms for bait. (I didn't!) He said that was all earthworms were good for—fish bait! Is that true?

Michael
Austin, Texas

Dear Michael,

Thank you for standing up for earthworms. You are right! Although earthworms are small and slimy, we are very important creatures. We are decomposers.

Earthworms eat dead stuff, break it down into nutrients, and return it back to the Earth. Plants use these nutrients for food. We also have the very important job of tunneling through soil and keeping it loose so plants can grow. You are right—we are more than fish bait!

Sincerely,
Professor Worm

GARDEN HAIKU

Planting, rain waters

Warm energizing sunlight

Sharing and working

Slimy worms squirming

Bees buzzing, seedlings sprouting

A thriving garden

Colorful flowers

Lettuce, green beans, cabbage, peas

A garden we share

—Ann Watanabe

The Garden We Share

by Myka-Lynne Sokoloff

illustrated by Tatjana Mai-Wyss

Chapter 1
A Perfect Place

Mama looked out the window and sighed. "That vacant lot is such a mess. Every time I look at it, it makes me sad," she said.

"Why don't we clean it up?" I asked.

"Oh, Cara. It's just too much work for the two of us," she said.

I was quiet, but my brain was busy. I came up with a splendid idea. "Mama, may I go to Josephine's?" I asked.

With Mama's permission, I scurried to my best friend's home and knocked on the door. I told Josephine my idea. "Cool!" she said.

What do you think Cara's splendid idea is?

53

I knew I could count on Josephine. We were so excited!

Josephine and I went up and down the block knocking on doors and ringing doorbells. We took turns telling the neighbors about our idea. They all thought it was an awesome plan!

The next Saturday, all the neighbors came out to help. I was impressed! Some had empty bags for trash. Other people carried rakes and shovels. Everyone got busy cleaning up the lot. We picked up empty bottles and scraps of paper. Then we raked the dirt so it was nice and smooth. The whole street looked so much better when we finished.

"It's so sunny here," said Mr. Phillips.

"This lot would be a great spot for growing tomatoes," said Mrs. Knight.

Why is the lot a great spot for growing tomatoes? What else does a plant need to grow?

54

We all agreed the lot would make a perfect place for a garden. Everyone said they would help.

Mr. Phillips said, "I have a hose."

"I have some seeds," said Mama.

"I have some extra tomato plants," added Mrs. Knight.

"This will be perfect," I thought.

Chapter 2
The Garden Thrives

Who is the story about?
What did the neighbors decide to do?

The neighbors helped turn the dirt, make rows, plant seeds, and water the plants. We set up a schedule for taking care of the garden.

In a few weeks, our community garden was thriving. Neat rows of lettuce grew like pretty green ribbons. Bean stalks curled up around old broom handles.

One day, as I was pulling weeds from the garden, I found some worms squirming in the dirt. I held one up to Josephine. "Ewww!" she shrieked. "I hate worms."

"Worms are good for our garden," explained Mrs. Chen. "They help make the soil soft so the roots can grow. They turn the dirt and make it airy so the roots can breathe."

I carefully put the worm back in the dirt and continued weeding.

As Josephine and I weeded, we noticed some rabbits sitting under a bush. They had one eye on us and one eye on the lettuce.

Everyone loved our garden in the lot. Butterflies and bees drank sweet nectar from the flowers. Robins ate worms. Other birds munched on beetles and ate sunflower seeds.

Why do you think the rabbits are interested in the garden?
Why did Cara carefully put the worm back in the garden?

SETTING

1. Where does the story take place?

MAIN CHARACTER, GOAL

2. Who is the main character, and what did she want?

ACTION

3. What was her "awesome plan"?

ACTION

4. What did the neighbors do?

INFERENCE

5. Why did Cara put the worm back?

DESCRIPTION

6. Describe the garden.

Chapter 3
Something for Everyone

Every day, the neighbors tended the garden. One day, we discovered that there were insects called aphids eating some of the plants. We could hardly see the tiny green bugs. "We should get rid of them," said Mrs. Knight. "Aphids make the plants weak."

"We can get some ladybugs," said Mrs. Chen. "Ladybugs eat aphids, and they won't eat our plants or harm anything else. I know exactly where to get ladybugs."

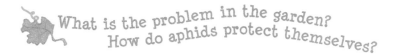

What is the problem in the garden? How do aphids protect themselves?

Mrs. Chen mailed away for the ladybugs. They came all wrapped up in a big ball. We let the ladybugs go in the garden. They chased around eating up the aphids. Soon our aphid problem was solved.

A few days later, we had a new problem. The rabbits had become bolder. They were making a feast of our lettuce and beans!

How did the gardeners solve their problem?
What is the new problem?
What do you think the gardeners should do?

"I have an idea," said Mr. Phillips. "We can build a fence around our garden."

Everyone got busy. The rabbits watched as we worked on the fence. Soon it was almost done.

"Wait," I said. "This garden is for the whole neighborhood. The people all enjoy it. So do the birds and butterflies. Could we leave a little piece of garden for the rabbits?"

We agreed to leave a little patch with no fence, so the rabbits could nibble on their own lettuce and beans.

Now we have a beautiful garden to harvest, and the rabbits have a little garden too. I like the garden we share.

What did the neighbors do to protect their garden? How did they share the garden with the rabbits? Do you think this was a good solution?

61

Fluency

Links in a Food Chain

Author Unknown
illustrated by Tatjana Mai-Wyss

There once was a flower that grew on the plain, 10
Where the sun helped it grow, and so did the rain, 21
Links in a food chain. 26

There once was a bug who nibbled on flowers, 35
Nibbled on flowers for hours and hours! 42

The bug ate the flower that grew on the plain, 52
Where the sun helped it grow, and so did the rain, 63
Links in a food chain. 68

There once was a bird who gobbled up bugs, 9
And creepies and crawlies and slimies and slugs. 17

The bird ate the bug who nibbled on flowers, 26
Nibbled on flowers for hours and hours! 33

The bug ate the flower that grew on the plain, 43
Where the sun helped it grow, and so did the rain, 54
Links in a food chain. 59

There once was a snake who often grabbed birds, 68
And swallowed them whole, or so I have heard. 77

The snake ate the bird who gobbled up bugs, 86
And creepies and crawlies and slimies and slugs. 94

The bird ate the bug who nibbled on flowers, 103
Nibbled on flowers for hours and hours! 110

The bug ate the flower that grew on the plain, 120
Where the sun helped it grow, and so did the rain, 131
Links in a food chain. 136

Fluency

There once was a fox, and I'll make a bet;   10
He'd eat anything he could possibly get.   17

The fox ate the snake who often grabbed birds,   26
and swallowed them whole, or so I have heard.   35

The snake ate the bird who gobbled up bugs,   44
And creepies and crawlies and slimies and slugs.   52

The bird ate the bug who nibbled on flowers,   61
Nibbled on flowers for hours and hours!   68

The bug ate the flower that grew on the plain,   78
Where the sun helped it grow, and so did the rain,   89
Links in a food chain.   94

The fox, he grew older and died one spring day,   10
But he made the soil rich when he rotted away.   20

A new flower grew where he died on the plain.   30
And the sun helped it grow, and so did the rain,   41
Links in a food chain.   46

This poem can be sung to the tune of *I Know an Old Woman Who Swallowed a Fly.*

Glossary

carnivore

A **carnivore** is an animal that eats mostly meat.

A wolf is a *carnivore*.

community

A **community** is a group of people or animals that live and work together.

The kids in our *community* like to work in the neighborhood garden.

connect

Connect means to join two or more things.

She *connected* the hose to the faucet.

decay

Decay means to rot.

The dead leaves were *decaying*.

decomposer

A plant or animal that helps dead matter rot, or decay, is called a **decomposer**.

An earthworm is a *decomposer*.

digest

When your body **digest** food, it breaks it down into energy that you can use.

Your stomach helps you *digest* food.

energy

Energy is the power to do things.

What gives plants the *energy* to grow?

floss

Floss means to clean between your teeth with a special thread.

The dentist always reminds us to *floss* our teeth.

food chain

A **food chain** is a group of plants and animals that are linked together. Each animal gets energy from another living thing in the chain.

Grass, zebras, and lions form a *food chain*.

herbivore

An **herbivore** is an animal that eats only plants.

A rabbit is an *herbivore*.

Glossary

link

A **link** is something that connects two things.

The rings in a chain are *links*.

nomadic

Nomadic describes people or animals that move around and do not stay in one place for very long.

Some American Indians lived a *nomadic* life because they followed the buffalo.

predator

A **predator** is an animal that hunts other animals for food.

A spider is a *predator* that kills and eats insects.

prey

Prey is an animal that is hunted and eaten by another animal.

A mosquito that is eaten by a bat is the bat's *prey*.

recycle

When you **recycle** something, it can be used again.

We *recycle* paper so it can be used again.

scarce

When something is **scarce**, there is not enough for everyone.

It hadn't rained for a long time, so water was *scarce*.

scurry

Scurry means to move quickly with small steps.

The little mouse *scurried* into its hole.

thrive

Thrive means to grow and do very well.

If you water a plant and give it sunlight, it will *thrive*.

thriving

Something that is **thriving** is growing exceptionally well.

The tomatoes we planted are *thriving* in the sunny garden.

unique

Unique means very special and one of a kind.

Each person has *unique* fingerprints.

Glossary

vacant

Vacant means empty. A building, a room, or even a chair can be vacant.

The house was *vacant.*

Idioms and Expressions

educated guess

An **educated guess** is not a wild guess. An educated guess is based on facts.

My cat eats mice, so I can make an *educated guess* that cats are carnivores.